"A delightfully creative and insightful book that teaches our kids that Christianity is not just about behavior change, but heart change, too."
J.D. GREEAR, PASTOR, THE SUMMIT CHURCH

"Simplifying biblical truth for children takes a lot of hard work, and Abbey has done it creatively, faithfully, and accessibly. *Your Amazing Hands* will help children to see the wonderful gospel story—and help parents to see gospel opportunities in everyday situations."
JANE WATKINS, GROWING YOUNG DISCIPLES

"I adore how Abbey has brought her distinctive, gospel-centered encouragement and equipping to this series! *Your Amazing Hands* is a fun, engaging read that kids and caregivers will reach for often. They'll find themselves slowly shaped to use their hands in a way that esteems the way Christ used his hands—to save us and bring us to himself."
CAROLINE SAUNDERS, AUTHOR, KIDS IN THE BIBLE

"The *Training Young Hearts* series is a favorite in our family. Abbey Wedgeworth packages big truths in bite-sized, understandable refrains that impact the hearts of children and their parents!"
GRETCHEN SAFFLES, WELL-WATERED WOMEN

"I trust Abbey's words and wisdom. I love thinking about these rich truths making their way into young hearts and minds."
DAVID THOMAS, AUTHOR, RAISING EMOTIONALLY STRONG BOYS

thegoodbook
for children

Your Amazing Hands
© Abbey Wedgeworth 2024.

Illustrated by Emma Randall | Design & Art Direction by André Parker

Published in association with The Gates Group

"The Good Book For Children" is an imprint of The Good Book Company Ltd
North America: thegoodbook.com UK: thegoodbook.co.uk Australia: thegoodbook.
com.au New Zealand: thegoodbook.co.nz India: thegoodbook.co.in

ISBN: 9781784989699 | JOB-007408 | Printed in India

WRITTEN BY
ABBEY WEDGEWORTH

ILLUSTRATED BY
EMMA RANDALL

YOUR AMAZING

HANDS

Your hands are **AMAZING!**
Your hands can **CLAP.**
They can high-five and wave!
They can **WIGGLE** and snap!

Your hands can **BUILD.**
They can throw,
dig, and hold!

Your hands can **CREATE** –
they can paint, stir, and mold!

Your hands **SQUEEZE** squirt bottles
and **VELCRO** your shoes...

and **BUTTON**
your buttons...

and **TIDY** your room!

They **SPLASH** and pick flowers,
make **MUD PIES** and **CAKES!**

And **FORTS** and sand-**CASTLES!**
And secret handshakes!

Your **FAN-TAS-TIC-AL** hands
can change someone's whole **DAY**
if you share yummy snacks
or beckon, "Come play!"

One **SQUEEZE** from your hand
could make someone feel **BRAVE!**
A few pats on the back
could drive sadness away!

since they're made by the God
who **CREATED** the **STARS!**

But our hands sometimes do
what God says we should **NOT**.
Like snatching or stealing
the things that we want.

Or **THROWING** in anger...

or **HITTING** to hurt...

or **POINTING** to blame...

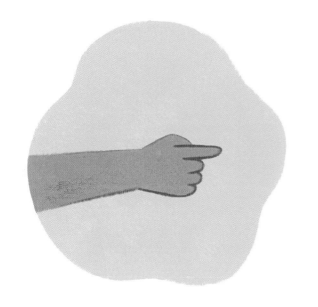

or **PUSHING** to be first.

But **GOD KNEW** we would not
use our hands like we should.
So he sent his Son, **JESUS,**
who did **ONLY** good!

He used **HIS** hands to heal,
to serve, and wash feet!

John 13 v 3-5

Luke 7 v 21

Matthew 8 v 1-3

John 6 v 5-13

He made one little lunch
food for **THOUSANDS** to eat!

His hands touched the folks
no one else would go near.
To kids **THEY** sent away,
HE said, "You're welcome here!"

More **AMAZING** than that,
because Jesus **LOVED** us,
he stretched his hands out
to be nailed to a **CROSS**.

Then he **ROSE** from the dead
and came out of that **TOMB**

so the power that **RAISED** him
could live inside **YOU!**

Now **HIS** Holy Spirit
gives you power to fight!
You can say **NO** to wrong!
You can do what is **RIGHT!**

So each time our hands fail
to do all God commands,
we can bow our heads,
we can **FOLD** our **HANDS**...

We can pray, "Lord, I'm sorry!"
and – right there and then! –
an **AMAZING** thing happens:
God forgives **ALL** our sin!

Then we open our hands
to ask for **HELP** to obey,
and God changes our hearts
so our hands choose **HIS** way.

Now put your hands together.
Shout, "Hip, hip, **HOORAY!**"
for the perfect hands of Jesus,
who'll make **US** like **HIM** one day.

And **NEVER** forget
   (no matter what **YOUR** hands do)
the way Jesus used **HIS** hands
      and still uses them... for **YOU!**

Follow Jesus' example and learn to rely on his amazing grace with
TRAINING YOUNG HEARTS

Rhyming books for ages 3+

Celebrate God's plan for our incredible bodies! These books inspire positive behavior and explore the amazing truth that Jesus was perfect *for* us. Look out for the next two books, all about mouths and eyes!

Lift-the-flap board books for toddlers

Simple, engaging, and practical, these books provide words to help you teach your kids about right and wrong actions, and point them to the gospel of grace.

 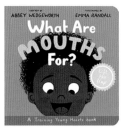  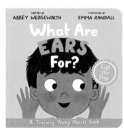

THEGOODBOOK.COM/TYH | THEGOODBOOK.CO.UK/TYH
THEGOODBOOK.COM.AU/TYH